Euphoria

Poems

F.S. Yousaf

Cover design by Wilder
Illustrations by Syed Saud

ISBN: 1983410365
ISBN-13: 978-1983410369

To Yusra & Eiman

7/12/17, 5:44 pm

You once told me that you disliked when I bought you flowers.

They live for a couple of days, then they die, and that hurts me.
Bring me a plant instead, so it can grow into something beautiful.

Fresh cut flowers are pleasant, but the happiness
That comes from maintaining and cherishing
An item with vulnerability
Seems to last longer.

Mistune

You told me
That you had made peace
With the consequences,
All I had to do was
Forgive myself
For all the things I had not done,
And to move on
As if we never even happened.

Return

I have ignored your messages,
Signs,
And constant reminders.
But I have fallen from grace
And I need you more than ever.
I vow to never forget you again.

Assured

I am always heard,
Even through silence.
As I write on paper
Or think to myself.
I am alone
But never forgotten.

Conform

Through abuse and hurt,
I was taught to stay silent.
My emotions were never to reach the surface,
they were to remain in the depths of my being
for letting them out would be unlawful.

"Masculinity"

Heaven

Soon
We will take over our own little world.
Filled with laughter,
Excitement,
Happiness,
Never any sorrow,
And everything we ever wished for.

Growth

The act of an apology
Does not hold the power to instantly heal,
But it gives enough momentum
To start moving forward.

The art of forgiveness

Lapse

I had not heard from you
In quite a while,
When you could hear me every day.
Begging for some sort of aid
When it was all I needed and craved.
You have said that patience is key,
But mine is running thin.

How long must I wait
Until I am allowed to become
Displeased by the way you have handled me?

Crisis

Heaven was made to hold the souls
that have done good on this earth,
and hell was made for the terrible
who terrorized the ground they laid their feet on.

Why could God not change their hearts,
when even he knew the sinister clouds
had billowed up in their bodies?
Were they so corrupt
that the almighty himself
became powerless in influencing their ways
for the better?

The way I sit becomes uncomfortable,
and my mind races relentlessly.
I question my existence and my whole being,
and wonder if I have truly gone mad.

Cherish

There is nothing more delightful
Than you, my love.
Even though you do not think so,
I hold you closer
Than anything else
That has entered my life.

Perception

I stare at my reflection to see
Who I have become.
I am a sloppy mold
Of past memories,
Present struggles,
And future worries.

Extract

A part of me left
When you said you wanted nothing to do with me.
That you were done trying,
Leaving me with no direction,
And I thought that missing part would end me.
I had felt so incomplete.

But I have been feeling different lately.
I have been content these last few days
And I am somewhat grateful
That you took some of my sadness with you.

Forsake

How much of a fool
I was
To have loved wholeheartedly
Without fearing
the outcome
Of no reciprocation.

Reminder

I see the way you love,
And know that I may never
Get that kind of treatment.
I am nothing
But a memory
Of the person
You despise the most.

Depart

Time will leave
Faster than
Anyone ever could,
And there is no chance
For it to come back.

Unease

The spontaneous nature
Or unknown aftermath of death
Does not scare me.
The uncomfortable emotion
That crawls up my spine
Is of leaving words unspoken,
And pain in those who adore me.

Journey

There are so many things
I would love to say to you.
So many questions I would
Love to ask you.
Call it closure in a way.

But God does not take for no reason.
And that was one of the hardest truths
I had to come to terms with.

That there was something better
Waiting for me,
But I just had to get past
The grueling,
Yet needed grace period.

Nightfall

The night had finally taken over.
No lights shined,
No stars glistened,
The wind was howling every other minute,
And the music of wind chimes filled my ears.
An odd night indeed

Does this night signify peace
And relaxation,
Or does this darkness foreshadow
Heartache and misfortune?

Heavy Heart

Slowly and slowly
You start seeing his pain act on his skin.
You start noticing his deathly movements when he is alone.
His dismal face,
His still mouth,
And those emotionless eyes.
His silent cries of help as he is locked up in his depressing
thoughts.
But no one else notices the agony he feels,
For he covers it with a smile.
A fake, dismal smile
That tends to fool everyone.

Relieved

I am thankful for the ones
that have seen the most of me,
and stayed.
I am thankful for the ones
Who left
Before knowing all of me.

Detrimental

I will care for you
In every possible way
I can,
But when your negativity
Starts to seep into my well being
That is when I have to
Let go.

Ambition

I do not desire a life

Where I am constructed by normality.

I crave a different life,

Something unlike others.

Disregard

The heart you carry
Resembles the concrete
On the ground.
Being walked all over
With no instinct or thought of it

Discover

I am lost
In my attempts to figure you out.
I desire no map,
Just to find all of you
With my very own will.

Deceitful

I cannot trust the way
You glance at me,
For you tell me tall tales
Of every kindhearted individual
that has entered your life.

I refuse to become
One of the many stories
In your book of deceptions.

Withstand

You have to promise me
That this is something
We will work on.
We will argue, we will fight,
But we must make sure
That it won't be the end of us.

Ignorance

Do you not believe
That we have endured enough
Hatred in history,
Just to bring it back once more
And stir up
Everything we thought was not possible?

Unmask

You memorized each
Of my weaknesses
As if they were your own.
Using them,
And lashing out at me
At the first drop
Of emotional distress.

Afterlife

The pain will deepen,
But the memories won't fade.
You are gone from this world,
But I know
You will be covered
In everlasting shade.

Snowfall

My love for you has withered
As winter has kissed
The beautiful roses
Our garden nested.

Oh father,
Can you not see
How much you have damaged
Our growth?
How you stole our dreams,
As well as our innocence?

My mind replays the events
Of five years prior.
When you rested,
And neglected
Every truthful statement
That was laid before
Your very eyes.

How dare the lack of love
Be blamed
On the person
Who cared for you the most.

My lies reminisce
Your tone,
But I know
That I do not resemble thee.

Your blood
Will run through
My body until it is no more.
Yet,
I am not the same man
As you.

That blood
Will keep the love alive
Between you and I.
But sadly,
Winter has arrived,
And the roses
Within me
Have died.

Al-Ala

When times seemed bleak
I questioned why
He was repeatedly testing me
consistently pushing me to the edge.

He was adding strength to my being,
and molding me into a better man

The Most High

Forgiveness

There are times when
I wanted the worst for you,
Hoping you would understand
The roots of my thoughts.
I needed you to feel the pain I held,
But here I am
Praying you never feel like I did.
Hoping no one ever sees you
Like the way you saw me.

Reluctant

If you know that I do not intend
To give up on us, what makes you
So terrified?

That anything can come in the way of us
The fear of it all crashing down
Is what I can't seem to let go of.

Wonderment

Ponder, my love.
Think about the trees,
The air,
The sky,
And its breeze.
Tell me this existence is not a theory,
But a miracle.

Wounds

Of course I love you too.
I loved you so much
that I'm not quite sure how possible
it is to love someone that much.
But we can't be together;
You're basically poison to me at this point.
You probably can't understand, but you will.
Maybe one day it'll work, but don't get
your hopes up and I won't either.

Trial

Your test for me
Was to see if I would raise my hands to you,
After I became distraught and confused.
To see if I would become stronger,
Or sulk in my depression.
You observed my doubt creeping,
And looked forward to my growth as a person.

Coping

My mental strains
have become a friend.
Someone who is always there
No matter the time or day.
Driving me mad,
And apologizing with happiness,
Moments
Or days later.

Mother

My motivation
Is created
To strive for
The woman
Who has given me life,
A house,
And a place to rest my head.
She was single handed,
Yet could achieve everything
A man could.

Raw

The way you have seen me
Is rarely witnessed by others.
I am bare-bodied,
My thoughts, aspirations, and love
Lay on the floor before you.

Craft

The sky awfully resembles human emotion.
Rain, fog, sunlight, and serenity,
Mesmerizing in all of its shades.
It is the art of god,
Like you and I.

Withstand

One of the only thoughts that can get me through a day

Is that whatever happens is meant to happen,

And for everything that leaves,

There is always something better on the way.

Journal Entries

To feel lost is natural,
In time
You will find yourself
Where you need to be,
And be more settled
Within your surroundings.

Al-Wasi

When we finally meet,
I hope that you will understand
Why I carried such negative emotions
Towards you.
And I hope that
You can take care of me,
And see that I would not carry these emotions
If I did not believe in you.

The All-Comprehending

Token

She is a reminder of my past,
A memento of sorts.
One that reminds me of my mistakes and imperfections.
My guilt latches on to the very image of her.
But she is also a reminder
That I am not that same person.
That there was always some good
within me.

Flourish

Hatred will not
Consume me,
For the good memories
Are still thriving within,
Even though
You have changed
So drastically.

Enchant

I had fallen for you,

But never realized that I had done so.

Everything about you was mesmerizing,

Like a summer's sunset,

Or a full moon on a clear night.

A perfect, beautiful distraction

To whatever I had felt.

Yearn

I dream of you, they are pleasant

And I feel at ease with the way

My mind has painted your being.

But when I wake,

I regret doing so.

Only because you are not next to me,

And too far for my hands to feel your skin.

Retaliate

The abuse that she endured
Had come back to rage against me.
I was forced to be a witness,
But could not tell
A single soul
What I had seen.

New Beginnings

Countries and oceans far away,
Our motherland rests.
She will not move,
But the children she bears
Will scatter throughout the world.
We are here,
In a new place and time,
We do not rest
In her cradle any longer.

Desire

She enlightened my mind, and softened my heart.
Her laugh was a killer,
The kind that added light to a dull afternoon.
She was caring,
And I envied that she beat my love for her tenfold.
She was exactly what people searched for,
And just what I needed.

Subtle Signs

My mother once told me,
Oh, so long ago,
that I would be destined for greatness,
But only by God's hand.
Through adversity and difficulties,
he would test me
to see if I was one,
or one with the many.

The lonesome nights had passed by
like a breeze on a calm night.
My prayer rug unfolded,
and hands cupped,
begging to give me strength,
even if it was just an ounce.
I beg for signs
over and over again.

Show me your greatness,
or leave me be.

The trees hunch over my window sill,
knocking as they please.
Reminding me that they are here,
and their presence will not go unnoticed.

Mislead

I am overwhelmed by how much
My thoughts toy with me.
Surrounded by love and support,
Yet believing
That I am utterly alone.

Torment

Breathable moments
Are only remembered
When anxiety has struck,
And has taken the privilege of air.
I am alone, grasping at my ribs,
Pleading myself to breathe,
As my mind has made me believe
That I am being suffocated
By the walls around me.

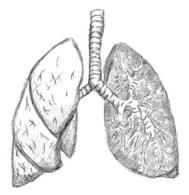

Drastic

You claim that your actions are out of love
And care,
Yet they seem extreme and outlandish
To even the people that know you.

Aspiration

Dreams of grandeur do not seduce me any longer.
Simplicity has become more attractive,
As I only desire a small area
of peace and happiness.

Gallery

My body is a museum,
As I am guided to memories and new pieces daily,
And to even the best kept secrets
Not known to mankind.
The reek of parchment and fresco fill the many rooms,
Freshly dried, and just written,
As I move along this empty palace.

Strength

I am sad, and it isn't the type of sadness to go away when
Things get better.
This sadness strikes at any moment, at any given time.
When I am riding high with family and friends,
I feel as if something latches onto me, and drags me to My
knees.
It holds me down and makes me suffer.
I become jailed by this sadness
And am occasionally freed.
Temporarily filled with joy and happiness,
Only to grow anxious, as I know it will make its return. Like
an earthquake,
If it does not strike often, it will hit with full force.
A week's worth of happiness
Becomes a night filled with intrusive,
And horrible thoughts.
I become incapacitated,
And know that if I give leverage to these thoughts,
I will lose.

I win when I do not fall victim to myself.
When I hold out till dawn,
And all the demons slip away into shadows.
This battle is constant,
And I fear one day I may lose, but that day is not today.

Lucidity

The mind is such an awfully dangerous place,
And I have to admit
That there are times
Where mine gets filled up with smoke
That I cannot seem to exhale.

You though,
You give me sense and clarity.

Y.S.

Siege

The demons have been coming back
Slowly breaking my aged wall.
Starting at dusk,
And leaving when first light settles in,
Giving me some time to harden the broken masterpiece.
As I struggle to keep up,
I see my once jubilant memories fleeing.

One by one the blocks will start to fall.
Should I let go of the wall,
They would all storm in,
And this fight would end quicker.

Should I support the ill-fated wall,
I would keep this temporary happiness
For just a little longer

Rouse

You make me feel
All the love
That I have lost
in my lifetime.

Without Faith, Who am I?

I am sorry,
for I have lost my innocence
to the world around me.
I did not wish for this,
but the feelings were just too immense
for me to ignore any longer.

Who have I become?
My mind clings onto hope.
I am starved
of something that I desire.

I have grown disheveled,
as if I am packed with animals
to the brim of a barn.
Restricted by the others
that are around me.

Am I the cause of tension?
If so, please voice your thoughts,
so I can sink through the ground below
and into a world of my own.
As long as a life eases,
my sacrifice will be worth it.

Who do I become
when I do not want to be myself?
I beg you to forgive the sins
that have built me from the ground up,
but even then
it all seems hopeless.

Come,
come with me.
Show me
what a true believer
is supposed to look like.

Uncertain

My hope lies within other people,
And I do not know
If this is a curse
Or a blessing.

Front

You would put any person over me,
If it meant that you would look better
For the world.
This truth was a simple one,
But difficult to grasp.

Struggle / Anticipation

I have not seen you
in a long time,
and though it kills me,
I know right now
it is for the better.

The miles separate us more
than arguments and fights.
I can read your words,
but cannot hear your voice.
I can hear your voice
but cannot see your face.
I can see your face,
and hear your voice,
but cannot touch your body.

As much as we put our differences aside,
we can only be so close.
My fingers cannot run through your hair,
and our bodies cannot mingle.
Our souls cannot dance,
intertwining together in foolish rhythms.

I long for the day I wake up
to your wholesome eyes,
and the ripeness that comes with you
after a long night.

Some time is needed
before our fate is decided,
but I know
you and I
will eventually come together.

Elongate

The night is all I have at times,
And I desperately try to make it last as much as I can.
I always feel like this is my final night on this earth
To just bask in its lifespan.

It never ends up being my last night,
And I wake dreading the mornings
Even more so.

Alongside

With her,
There were times when loneliness
Would strike,
And she would be there,
Doing her best to be the comfort to my distress.
She had never experienced these emotions,
As she would only feel them second-hand.

Without her,
I was alone most of the time
And could only bear the pain
Until its eventual passing.

Fictitious Reflection

Walking around the starlit park,
A cool breeze flows over us.
No noise all around
Lamps lit, it looks almost like daylight out.
And we are just in our own little world.

We stop next to a big tree
Leaves colored with the turning of Fall.
I gently touch her arms as they sit in her fancy coat,
We turn and look at each other.
The dark, eerie water calmly moves behind her.
I am staring right into her eyes
I wanted to believe that she was the one,
That we would be together for a long time.
I always tend to get ahead of myself at the worst possible
moments.

But I could see right past her fake laugh and smile,
Seeing that she was still in love.
She was stuck in the past,
Thinking about all the memories that she held of him,
Only to know that he wasn't there anymore.
He broke her ever so dearly,
But she was still longing for his touch,
Not mine.
I wasn't the one that was for her,
I was a person she wouldn't see herself with.
She already made up her mind.

Her laugh was shallow and her eyes cried of sorrow.
She would not try to keep this going,
I could see it.
For she was talking to me, but thinking of him.

Prayers

Sometimes all we have left are prayers to God.
Situations escape from our grasps,
And we are left physically hopeless.

The hope lies within our words,
Which are carried by the wind to the unknown.
Maybe they enter someone else's mind,
Or land in a pile of prayers,
That mercilessly stack in front of God.
They sit, waiting to be answered right away,
In time, or never.

The pleasure is not ours to know.
I have nothing left besides these words I speak to you, And I
hope you get them in due time.

Enough

My heart swells
Under the pressure
Of not being enough.
But she reminds me
Time and time again
That no one else
Could complete her
Like I do.

Forged

I was carefully crafted

From both of your structures.

All the flaws and pieces of good

Built within me.

Realizations

Behind the door,
in the dimly lit room,
There sits a boy
doubting everything he has been told
since he was a child
in his father's cradle.

God judges by intention,
and it should not matter
who you hurt,
as long as you pray
and read the holy scripture.

Make mistakes,
beat people beyond recognition,
but as long as your intention
of not doing any harm is there,
God has cleared you from sin,
and the gates of heaven are still at your footsteps.

Your words have taught me well,
and your terrible actions have too.
I hope I am in heaven one day,
with or without you.

Nowadays

I trek home,

through rain,

snow,

mud,

and sorrow.

I enter a home

where silence greets me,

and the skeleton

of happiness

glooms over me.

What used to be

Fondness

I do not have much to offer you,
Barely anything if I must speak the truth.
With every wish at your fingertips,
Why do you still show care
To a simple man like myself?

Toxicity

I staunchly believed
That my heart
Was the purist
Out of everyone I had encountered.
But no one thinks they are
Ever the bad guy.
Just the misunderstood.

Exist

I am tired of worrying

Over the expanding tension

That resides in me.

Let me live a little

Before I collapse.

Disloyal

She was there through
All your pain and suffering,
And every challenge and test,
Yet you betrayed her.
Afterwards, you showered her with
Half-hearted apologies.
She deserved so much more
Than a half-made man.

Ramadan

The day has come,
which marks the end
of a month
that carried holiness.

I am riddled with guilt.
My actions do not deserve
of being blessed.
I do not feel forgiven
for the many sins I have committed.

In the beginning,
I said this would be different.
That I would attain
spiritual bliss,
unlike the many other months.

The nights were young.
I remember being rocked
back and forth
to wake up
for morning prayers.
I could not,
So I stayed up.

My eyes are closed,
yet my mind is awake.
My body is limp,
yet it is taking shape.

I am awake.
Prayer starts in five minutes,
and yet I cannot find the time
to talk to the most high.

I was the only one
who did not cry.
I did not beg,
I did not whimper.
I stood,
stone faced,
hoping that one day
I would be forgiven.

I did cry once.
My mind was in pain,
my notebook soaked.
I did not deserve
the world I was in,
or even being pardoned.
I cried into the air,
and still felt nothing.

Emptiness.
Solitude.
What a blessing.

Liberated

As much as it hurt
To see you leave,
It could not compare to the feeling
Of finally being free.

When you left

Unparalleled

No matter what I did,
You never gave up on me.
You had my back,
Supporting me through every decision.
Believing in me,
And not being afraid
To tell me the truth
When I needed it the most.
You were the first woman in my life,
And the only person
That can never be replaced.

Coax

The devil whispered into my ear
That I was young and strong,
Maybe even indestructible.
That I could procrastinate my beliefs
Since time was by my side.
I was someone who could not die.

I must constantly remind myself
That no one is guaranteed tomorrow.

Kismet

When I looked into your eyes,
I did not see stars,
Galaxies,
Or anything out of the blue.
I only saw the love, the passion
That any other man could have had,
But only I was lucky enough to.

Indebted

You were irreplaceable,
As our blood had me bound.
Even after your departure,
A speck of love remained,
Yearning for what it had lost.

I met someone
Along my path
Who gave me
Something that certainly
Made up for your absence.

a family

Compiled

My weak thoughts
Accumulated into something vicious,
Tearing me up
From the inside out.

Tranquility

As long as you keep on smiling,
My heart will be at ease.
Though we are not meant
For each other,
Your happiness still
Means the world to me.

Clean Slate

The past behind us

A fresh start

A familiar face

Positive thoughts

And nothing holding us back.

Fuse

Maybe we were made of the same material,
Or we were just two different people
Trying to make something
That could not blend.

Radiant

The world rarely falls apart.
Everything feels sturdy and in place
For the first time in a long time.
So long that I have forgotten
The feeling of being content.
Things are finally looking up,
Things may finally change.

Self-Improvement

Tell me when you are gone

For good,

So I can

Finally start

Working on myself.

Reawakened

It has only been a short while,
But I feel as if
I have grown exponentially.
Reborn within my own flesh,
Igniting from various struggles
That I did not expect.

Alter

Our love faded
Once the mask came off
And your true colors
Flourished.

Salaam

I owe you no words,
No courtesies,
And not a single beat of my heart.
Nothing.

But I wish you peace
Despite all of our differences.

Alleviate

Your choices in life
Do not bother me
Any longer.
You are a free being;
I can only hope
You are guided.

Reticent

I ponder over how much
You care for me
When you would rather
Let silence speak on our behalf,
Than find ways to bind
Our differences.

Fortify

I have to constantly reinforce
That I will be okay,
No matter what happens in life
Or what terrible thoughts cross my mind.
I am exhausted,
Repeatedly repelling
The madness every day.

10/12/17, 12:25 AM

Forbearance

I am aware

That you look at everyone else,

Aching to do the things we cannot.

I promise that in time

We will get to.

Caught

Riches and materials,
Items that do not mean a thing.
Fulfilling desires
And never being content.
Halted happiness,
And completely losing myself
In this world.

Loops

Let me think of the reasons,
But I cannot come up with one.
Why you are still resting in my mind
When I am praying at night.

You happen to find your way
Into my words.
And at two in the morning,
When I cannot sleep,
You are all I can think about.
It's a repeated cycle that I cannot ignore.

I am writing a one-sided story.

Blessings

He does not take away
And leave your hands empty.
In times of struggle and loss,
We tend to believe
That we must fend for ourselves.
But He is watching
And giving us more
Than we could ever ask for.

We tend to forget that we are not alone
Feb. 9, 2016

Overthought

I became so scared of the future,
That I forgot about the present.

I became so worried of judgement,
That I completely changed myself
To someone who I was not.

I became so scared of the fear
That I lost focus on life itself.

Rise

The sun will rise through the ashes
Of the night,
And it will bring a new feeling for us.

We will know that all the struggles
Only made us stronger.

Unprepared

The cold was nothing new to me.
The breeze would hurt my lungs,
Stiffen my fingers,
And numb my ears.
Yet I could find a way to keep warm.

Except your frigidness
Was new to me,
And I was without a clue
On how to handle it.

Tawakkul

Somehow the moonlight
Seemed brighter
The night we forgave one another
And left all of our fate
To the most high.

Trusting God's plan

Maturation

I did not know
How to live normally
Until you were gone,
And your absence struck me
As if I had experienced a death.

Throughout time,
I slowly learned
To love who I was,
So I would not crave it from anyone.

A Tale of Euphoria

I have been told many times
That happiness is temporary,
So much so that the statement has ingrained itself
Into my daily thoughts.

But if others would cease to throw me down
When I am at a clear high,
Then perhaps my euphoria
Would last a bit longer.

Made in the USA
Las Vegas, NV
18 October 2020